BUILDING BRIDGES AND ROADS
CIVIL ENGINEERS

AMY HAYES

PowerKiDS press.

New York

Published in 2016 by The Rosen Publishing Group, Inc.
29 East 21st Street, New York, NY 10010

First Edition

Editor: Caitlin McAneney
Book Design: Katelyn Heinle/Tanya Dellaccio

Photo Credits: Cover ImagesBazaar/Getty Images; cover (background) Lev Kropotov/Shutterstock.com; cover, pp. 4–30 (gear vectors) Hunor Olah/Shutterstock.com; p. 5 (pyramids) Dan Breckwoldt/Shutterstock.com; p. 5 (Great Wall of China) Hung Chung Chih/Shutterstock.com; p. 6 iofoto/Shutterstock.com; p. 7 Kunal Mehta/Shutterstock.com; p. 8 Andrey Bayda/Shutterstock.com; p. 9 hxydl/Shutterstock.com; pp. 11 (drawing), 30 Fernando Blanco Calzada/Shutterstock.com; p. 11 (Brooklyn Bridge) kan_khampanya/Shutterstock.com; p. 13 microvector/Shutterstock.com; p. 14 https://commons.wikimedia.org/wiki/File:Joseph_Strauss_Memorial.jpg; p. 15 Martin M303/Shutterstock.com; p. 17 (New York City) Songquan Deng/Shutterstock.com; p.17 (architects) Dragon Images/Shutterstock.com; p. 19 Robert Cernohlavek/Shutterstock.com; p. 21 turtix/Shutterstock.com; p. 23 William Perugini/Shutterstock.com; p. 25 (glowing lines) Remko De Waal/Stringer/Getty Images; p. 25 (wind turbines) Moschen/Shutterstock.com; p. 27 (top) wavebreakmedia/Shutterstock.com; p. 27 (bottom) Hero Images/Getty Images; p. 29 Goodluz/Shutterstock.com.

Library of Congress Cataloging-in-Publication Data

Hayes, Amy, author.
 Building bridges and roads : civil engineers / Amy Hayes.
     pages cm. — (Engineers rule!)
 Includes index.
 ISBN 978-1-5081-4532-5 (pbk.)
 ISBN 978-1-5081-4533-2 (6 pack)
 ISBN 978-1-5081-4534-9 (library binding)
 1. Civil engineering—Juvenile literature. 2. Bridges—Design and construction—Juvenile literature. 3. Sky-scrapers—Design and construction—Juvenile literature. I. Title. II. Series: Engineers rule!
 TA149 .H3285
 624—dc23
                                        2015036124

Manufactured in the United States of America

CPSIA Compliance Information: Batch #BW16PK: For Further Information contact Rosen Publishing, New York, New York at 1-800-237-9932

CONTENTS

THE WORLD OF CIVIL ENGINEERING

Have you ever wondered what keeps a bridge from falling down or makes a tunnel's ceiling stay up? Have you thought about the pipes that run under cities and towns or how buildings can stretch high into the sky? Have you ever seen a whole river or lake being held back by a dam and wondered how it was built? The engineers who work on the roads, buildings, and foundations we depend on are called civil engineers.

Go on a walk and look at all the amazing structures under your feet and over your head. Whether it's a house or a skyscraper, a highway or a small bridge on a country road, you can bet a civil engineer helped build it.

Civil engineering is one of the oldest forms of engineering. It began with ancient civilizations. The pyramids in Egypt and the Great Wall of China have something in common with today's roads and skyscrapers—they were designed by a talented group of engineers!

PYRAMIDS IN EGYPT

GREAT WALL OF CHINA

ENGINEERING THE ROADS AND RAILS

There are several different types of civil engineers. A transportation engineer is a person who specializes in making sure people can travel in the safest, most **efficient** ways possible. This means they design all sorts of roads and paths, from highways to railroads.

Transportation engineers make sure roads are built according to safety guidelines. To do this, they use a lot of math and a branch of science called **physics**. This allows them to predict how fast the cars can safely go depending on how **abruptly** the road turns. They also decide how many lanes there should be. They can even determine how traffic jams will start and come up with ways to prevent them.

Railroads have to be designed by engineers, too. It's very important to make sure trains stay on the tracks.

Roads have been around a lot longer than engineers. So when did people decide it was a good idea to get civil engineers involved? Once cars became popular, roads became much more **dangerous**. People on horseback traveled at much slower speeds than people driving cars. Cars presented new problems that needed solutions.

In 1921, the state of Ohio created the first state Traffic Engineering Bureau in the country. They hired Harry E. Neal to help organize and number the highways in the state. Soon, Neal developed a plan to draw lines on the road to prevent cars from crashing into each other. The idea of hiring people to create rules for the road with signs, lines, and speed limits spread across the country.

Cars were the reason that civil engineers got involved with creating roads. Now every road has to be carefully planned to make sure it's safe.

STRUCTURAL ENGINEERING

Structural engineers work on all kinds of large projects, including buildings and dams. One of their specialties is creating bridges. Roads can get you quite far, but what if you have to cross a river or a lake? Structural engineers work with **architects** and construction workers to make sure any bridge that's built can withstand great amounts of weight.

Structural engineers have to know a lot about materials—how strong they are and how they react under different conditions. Structural engineers have a good understanding of physics and chemistry, two branches of science. They also have to use math every day as they perform important calculations that deal with the size of their structure and how the weight of its users and the pull of gravity will affect it.

Structural engineers think about what kind of bridge design would be safest. They have to think about how many people will be crossing the bridge and how long it will be.

BROOKLYN BRIDGE

Four major kinds of bridges are beam, truss, arch, and suspension. A beam bridge has a long, flat beam that vehicles drive over from end to end. It's supported by the two ends and sometimes poles underneath. A truss bridge usually has a series of steel bars assembled into triangle units.

The arch bridge has a big curve underneath its flat surface. The arch rises up towards the center and slopes down to either side. These lower ends hold the weight of the bridge. The last kind of bridge is a suspension bridge. It has tall towers with wires that come down and hold the bridge deck in place. Each bridge has different advantages and disadvantages. Structural engineers always work hard to figure out what kind of bridge they need to build.

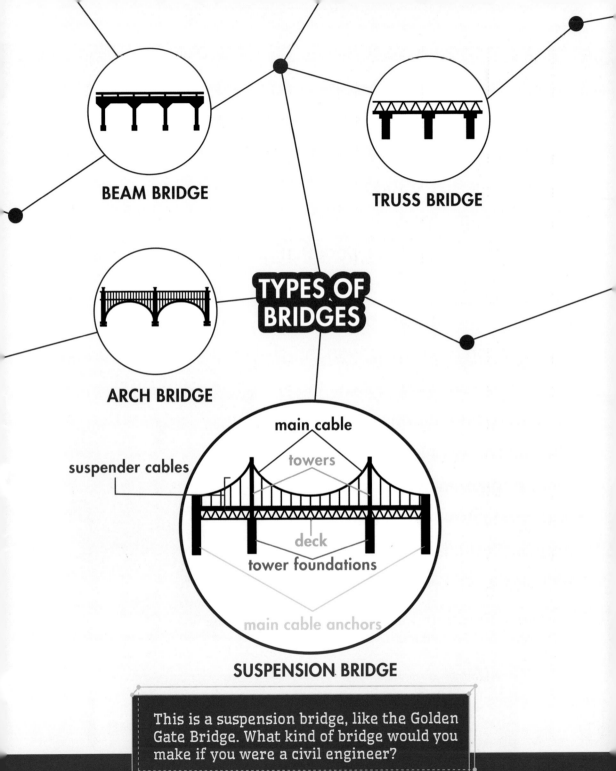

BEAM BRIDGE

TRUSS BRIDGE

ARCH BRIDGE

TYPES OF BRIDGES

main cable

suspender cables

towers

deck

tower foundations

main cable anchors

SUSPENSION BRIDGE

This is a suspension bridge, like the Golden Gate Bridge. What kind of bridge would you make if you were a civil engineer?

THE GOLDEN GATE BRIDGE

The Golden Gate Bridge is one of the most famous bridges in the world. It's 8,981 feet (2,737.4 m) long and weighs over 887,000 tons (804,672.9 mt). On the first day the bridge opened, over 200,000 people walked on the bridge to see all the work that had been done. It's six lanes wide with two sidewalks, one on either side, totaling 90 feet (27.4 m) across.

Joseph B. Strauss was the civil engineer who worked on the Golden Gate Bridge. He designed the suspension bridge after talking with a trusted board of other engineers. It was approved, and soon work began on the new bridge. It took four years of work by hundreds of people before the bridge opened in 1937.

STATUE OF JOSEPH B. STRAUSS

The Golden Gate Bridge is held up by a series of very strong wires that are suspended from thick cables that cross the tops of the towers. This is why it's called a suspension bridge.

JOSEPH B. STRAUSS

Joseph B. Strauss was born in Cincinnati, Ohio, on January 9, 1870. He graduated from the University of Cincinnati in 1892 and worked as an **apprentice** draftsman, or person who makes technical plans for structures. In the 1920s, he helped design and lead the project to work on what would become the longest bridge in the world. Though it held that title only until the 1960s, the Golden Gate Bridge is still the symbol of the great city of San Francisco.

BUILDING SKYSCRAPERS

Structural engineers don't just build bridges—they also create buildings. Look at a picture of the skyline of New York City. Structural engineers played a large part in building those huge skyscrapers.

When a structural engineer works on a big project such as a skyscraper, they need to communicate with many other workers. They work with the architect who's designing the layout of the building. They also work with geotechnical engineers to make sure the ground is safe to build on.

Before construction is started, the structural engineer makes sure the building will have a strong enough foundation to support the weight of the structure. They need to keep the force of wind in mind for skyscrapers and, in some areas, the risk of earthquakes.

Structural engineers use a lot of math and physics to ensure their building is safe. They consider the weight of the building itself and also its live load—the weight of the people and objects that will be placed in and on it.

NEW YORK CITY

GEOTECHNICAL ENGINEERING

Building roads, bridges, and buildings can only be successful if the ground beneath them is able to support the structure. The quality of soil or rock underneath and around a structure plays a big part in its ability to hold weight and last a long time. Geotechnical engineers are called before construction starts. "Geo" means "earth," and geotechnical engineers are the technical experts of the ground and the earth.

First, these engineers inspect the ground and make sure the area is safe enough to construct a building, tunnel, or **reservoir**. They can even improve the ground by treating the soil. They also look at risks, such as the chance of a landslide or earthquake in an area. Geotechnical engineers have to use geology, the science of Earth, to do their job.

Geotechnical engineers make sure the ground is strong enough to hold up a building without caving in.

TUNNELING THROUGH

Tunnels are some of the most difficult things civil engineers have to work on. Engineers have to be very familiar with physics before beginning work on a tunnel. Before starting a tunnel, geotechnical engineers learn as much as they can about the soil and rocks workers will be digging through. They also have to know what kind of tunnel they're making: Is it for cars to drive through or people to walk through?

RUNNING WATER

If you live in a place that has running water, you know how easy it is to **access** it. Starting a bath, brushing your teeth, or just getting a cool glass of water to drink is a turn of the knob away. However, none of this would be possible without water-supply engineers. Water-supply engineers make sure that there's enough water for a community and that the water is safe to drink.

Water-supply engineers have to study several branches of science to be able to handle the difficult jobs they have to do. They study hydrology, or the science of water; meteorology, the study of weather; geology; and **environmental** science. With their knowledge, water-supply engineers work to make sure there's enough clean water for the public to use.

Water-supply engineers work with other engineers to create reservoirs and dams. They ensure that as much water as possible is conserved so it can be used by the community.

THE HOOVER DAM

One of the most well-known dams in the world is the Hoover Dam. It stands over 726 feet (221.3 m) high. Civil engineer Frank Crowe was the head engineer on the project, and with 21,000 workers, it took four years to complete. When the Hoover Dam was finished, it created Lake Mead. The Hoover Dam prevents floods, and Lake Mead provides water for farms and is a major water supply for Los Angeles, California, and several other cities.

CONSTRUCTION ENGINEERS

Construction engineers manage construction projects. They take a look at everything that architects and other engineers have put together—the design of what's going to be constructed. Then, they have to make sure that everything is put together exactly the way the designs specify.

Being a construction engineer is exciting but difficult work. Communication is an important skill for construction engineers—they have to make sure their workers understand what they're supposed to do. They also have to ensure everyone on the work **site** is safe. They spend a lot of time coming up with safe, temporary structures called scaffolding that can be put up quickly to help workers do their job and then taken down once the job is finished. Construction engineers also make sure structures are built on time.

The job of the construction engineer is to make sure that new buildings are designed according to plans and that scaffolding and other structures are safe to work on.

THE FUTURE OF CIVIL ENGINEERING

Civil engineering is an exciting career that will only continue to grow. Civil engineers are now facing important challenges: how to make new projects **sustainable** and how to incorporate energy conservation into everything they do.

As civil engineers start to address these issues, there will be more **collaboration** and teamwork needed. Civil engineers will have to work with mechanical engineers and electrical engineers to come up with creative solutions for basic everyday problems. Some of this collaboration is already happening. Civil engineers are starting to work with electrical engineers to come up with roads that can light up on their own or even act as solar panels. Some even want highways that incorporate wind turbines to power lights with the wind that cars create as they pass by.

Smart highways tackle problems with really exciting solutions, such as paint that glows in cold weather or wind turbines that light the area cars are driving through. Engineers working together will make for a bright and exciting future!

FIRST STEPS TO BECOMING A CIVIL ENGINEER

Now that you know what civil engineers do, maybe you want to build buildings or construct roads, tunnels, or even bridges. What does it take to be a civil engineer?

First things first: study hard! Engineers have to go to college, which means scoring well on tests and doing a lot of homework. All future engineers should be experts in STEM, or science, technology, engineering, and math. Your science and math classes will prepare you for engineering in the future. It also helps to be interested in how machines and structures work. Doing science experiments outside of class and signing up for after-school activities that deal with science and math will prepare you to solve problems and think on your feet.

School is an opportunity to find out what your interests are and explore them!

ON YOUR WAY!

After high school, potential civil engineers attend special programs specific to engineering. Some of these are technical schools, while others are colleges that have specific coursework provided for engineers. Once you start your engineering coursework, you can focus on civil engineering.

When training to be an engineer, a student may have **internships** and co-ops in college. Co-op education is when a student is paid to work for a company and learn as much as he or she can, but it isn't a permanent job. Different colleges require a different number of co-ops. Co-ops provide important experiences and give future engineers connections so they can find a job. Once a student graduates, they apply to jobs and are hired to work as a civil engineer.

Many civil engineering students keep going to school after they graduate with their bachelor's, or four-year, degree. They get advanced degrees in engineering so they're experts on the subject.

DESIGNING THE WORLD

Civil engineers have important jobs—they build the structures that we need to live, work, and travel. From tunnels underground, to skyscrapers that reach towards the clouds, civil engineers have shaped cities, towns, and everywhere in between.

The first **priority** of a civil engineer is making things as safe as possible. They aim to use materials that are good quality and safe for the environment. They listen to the needs of their customers and the community to develop the best structures possible. Civil engineers come up with remarkable designs that are both useful and pleasing to the eye. As the world

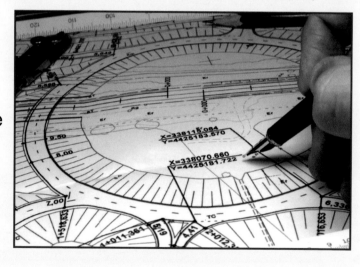

faces new challenges, civil engineers will be at the forefront, inventing and designing a better world.

GLOSSARY

abruptly: Very suddenly.

access: The ability to get or use something.

apprentice: Someone who learns a trade by working with a skilled person of that trade.

architect: A person who designs buildings.

collaboration: The action of working together to achieve a goal.

dangerous: Unsafe.

efficient: Producing desired effects with as little waste as possible.

environmental: Having to do with the natural world.

internship: An educational or training program that gives experience for a career.

physics: The study of matter, energy, force, and motion, and the relationship among them.

priority: Something that is more important than other things and needs to be dealt with first.

reservoir: A collection of water usually held back by a dam.

site: A place where a building stands or where something is being built.

sustainable: Able to last a long time.

INDEX

WEBSITES

Due to the changing nature of Internet links, PowerKids Press has developed an online list of websites related to the subject of this book. This site is updated regularly. Please use this link to access the list: www.powerkidslinks.com/engin/civil